MASTERING EXPENSE TRACKING AND BUDGETING APPS: AUTOMATED TRACKING AND FINANCIAL PLANNING

Table of Contents
1. Introduction
2. Chapter 1: The Challenges of Managing Finances
3. Chapter 2: What Are Expense Tracking and Budgeting Apps?
4. Chapter 3: Benefits of Using Expense Tracking and Budgeting Apps
5. Chapter 4: Choosing the Right Expense Tracking and

Budgeting App
6. **Chapter 5: Setting Up Your Financial App**
7. **Chapter 6: Effective Expense Tracking**
8. **Chapter 7: Mastering Budgeting**
9. **Chapter 8: Advanced Features and Customization**
10. **Chapter 9: Maintaining Your Financial Health**
11. **Conclusion**
12. **Appendix**

INTRODUCTION

Understanding the Importance of Expense Tracking and Budgeting

In today's fast-paced world, managing personal finances can be a daunting task. Many people struggle to keep track of their spending, set realistic budgets, and achieve their financial goals. This eBook, "Mastering Expense Tracking and Budgeting Apps: Automated Tracking and Financial Planning," aims to provide a comprehensive guide to overcoming these challenges using modern financial tools.

The Rise of Digital Financial Tools

The advent of digital technology has revolutionized the way we manage our finances. Expense tracking and budgeting apps have emerged as powerful tools that offer automated tracking, real-time updates, and personalized financial insights. These apps simplify the process of managing money, making it easier for users to stay on top of their finances and make informed financial decisions.

CHAPTER 1: THE CHALLENGES OF MANAGING FINANCES

Difficulty Tracking Expenses

One of the primary challenges people face in managing their finances is keeping track of their expenses. With numerous daily transactions, it can be difficult to remember where money is being spent and to maintain accurate records. This can lead to overspending, missed bill payments, and a general sense of financial chaos.

Tracking expenses manually can be time-consuming and error-prone. It often involves keeping receipts, writing down purchases, and entering data into spreadsheets. This process is not only tedious but also increases the risk of human error. Without an efficient system in place, it's easy to lose track of expenses, leading to financial disorganization.

Struggles with Budgeting

Creating and sticking to a budget is another common challenge. Many people find it hard to set realistic spending limits and often end up overspending in certain categories, which can lead to financial stress and debt. Budgeting requires discipline and a clear understanding of income and expenses, but many individuals lack the tools and knowledge to create effective budgets.

A well-constructed budget is essential for financial stability. It helps allocate resources efficiently, ensuring that necessary expenses are covered while also setting aside money for savings and investments. However, without proper guidance and tools, the budgeting process can feel overwhelming, leading many to abandon their budgets altogether.

Lack of Financial Awareness

Without a clear understanding of their financial situation, individuals may make poor financial decisions. This lack of awareness can prevent them from saving effectively, investing wisely, and achieving long-term financial goals. Financial awareness involves knowing where your money is going, understanding your financial habits, and being aware of your overall financial health.

Many people operate on autopilot when it comes to their finances, making purchases without considering the long-term impact on their financial health. This lack of awareness can result in accumulating debt, insufficient savings, and missed opportunities for investment. Developing financial awareness is crucial for making informed decisions that contribute to financial well-being.

CHAPTER 2: WHAT ARE EXPENSE TRACKING AND BUDGETING APPS?

Definition and Overview

Expense tracking and budgeting apps are digital tools designed to help users manage their finances more effectively. These apps offer features such as automated expense tracking, budget creation, and financial reporting, making it easier to monitor spending and achieve financial goals. By providing a centralized platform for financial management, these apps simplify the process of tracking expenses and managing budgets.

These apps connect to users' bank accounts and credit cards, automatically recording transactions and categorizing expenses. This eliminates the need for manual data entry and ensures that all transactions are accounted for. Additionally, they provide visual representations of spending patterns, helping users understand where their money is going.

Key Features of Financial Apps

CHAPTER 3: BENEFITS OF USING EXPENSE TRACKING AND BUDGETING APPS

Automated Expense Tracking

One of the biggest advantages of using financial apps is the ability to track expenses automatically. By linking bank accounts and credit cards, transactions are recorded in real-time, eliminating the need for manual entry and reducing the risk of errors. This ensures that all expenses are accurately tracked, providing a comprehensive view of financial activity.

Automated expense tracking also allows users to categorize transactions, making it easier to see how money is being spent. This categorization helps identify spending patterns and areas where adjustments can be made. Additionally, the real-time nature of automated tracking ensures that users always have up-to-date information on their finances.

Simplified Budgeting

Budgeting becomes much easier with the help of these apps. Users can set up budgets for various categories, receive alerts when they are close to their limits, and adjust budgets based on spending habits and financial goals. This helps ensure that spending is controlled and aligned with financial objectives.

The ability to set up and manage budgets in an app provides a structured approach to financial management. Users can allocate funds to different categories, such as housing, food, and entertainment, and monitor their spending against these allocations. The app provides visual representations of budget progress, helping users stay on track and avoid overspending.

Enhanced Financial Awareness

Financial apps provide detailed insights into spending patterns, helping users become more aware of their financial habits. This increased awareness can lead to better financial decisions and improved financial health. By understanding where money is going, users can make informed choices about their spending and saving.

Financial awareness is crucial for achieving financial goals. By using an app to track expenses and monitor budgets, users gain a clearer understanding of their financial situation. This awareness enables them to make proactive decisions, such as cutting back on unnecessary expenses or increasing contributions to savings and investments.

CHAPTER 4: CHOOSING THE RIGHT EXPENSE TRACKING AND BUDGETING APP

Assessing Your Needs

Before selecting a financial app, it is important to assess your specific needs. Consider factors such as your financial goals, the complexity of your finances, and the features you require. For example, if you need help with budgeting, look for an app that offers robust budgeting features. If you want to track investments, choose an app that includes investment tracking capabilities.

Understanding your financial needs will help you select an app that aligns with your goals. Some apps are better suited for individuals with simple finances, while others offer advanced features for more complex financial situations. Take the time to evaluate your needs and choose an app that provides the tools and functionality you require.

Comparing Popular Apps

There are many expense tracking and budgeting apps available, each with its own strengths and weaknesses. Popular options include Mint, YNAB (You Need A Budget), PocketGuard, and Personal Capital. Compare these apps based on features, ease of use, and cost to find the best fit for your needs.

Consider reading reviews and trying out free trials to see which app works best for you. Each app has its own interface and user experience, so it's important to find one that you find intuitive and easy to use.

Cost Considerations

Financial apps come with various pricing models, from free versions with limited features to premium subscriptions. Consider your budget and the value that the app will bring to your financial management when making a decision. Free apps may offer basic features, while premium apps provide more advanced tools and support.

Evaluate the cost of the app against the benefits it provides. A premium app may have a higher upfront cost, but the features and support it offers could lead to significant improvements in your financial management. Consider whether the additional features justify the cost and whether the app will help you achieve your financial goals.

CHAPTER 5: SETTING UP YOUR FINANCIAL APP

Creating an Account

The first step in setting up a financial app is creating an account. This typically involves providing basic information and choosing a subscription plan if applicable. Follow the prompts to set up your profile, including entering your name, email address, and other necessary details.

Once your account is created, take the time to explore the app's interface and familiarize yourself with its features. Most apps offer tutorials or guides to help you get started. Understanding the layout and functionality of the app will make it easier to use effectively.

Linking Bank Accounts and Credit Cards

To start tracking expenses automatically, link your bank accounts and credit cards to the app. This process is usually straightforward and secure, allowing the app to access transaction data in real-time. Follow the app's instructions to link your accounts, which may involve entering login credentials for your financial institutions.

Linking your accounts is a crucial step in automating expense tracking. It ensures that all transactions are recorded accurately and provides a comprehensive view of your financial activity. Most apps use secure encryption methods to protect your data, so you can link your accounts with confidence.

Customizing Categories and Budgets

Once your accounts are linked, customize the spending categories and set up budgets for each one. This will help you track your spending more accurately and stay within your budget limits. Adjust the default categories to match your spending habits and create new categories as needed.

Setting up budgets involves allocating specific amounts to each category. Review your past spending to determine realistic budget limits. The app will track your spending against these limits and provide alerts when you are approaching or exceeding your budget. Customizing categories and budgets ensures that the app reflects your financial reality.

CHAPTER 6: EFFECTIVE EXPENSE TRACKING

Recording Expenses Automatically

With your financial app set up, expenses will be recorded automatically from your linked accounts. This eliminates the need for manual entry and ensures that all transactions are accounted for. The app will categorize transactions based on merchant information and spending patterns.

Automatic expense tracking provides a real-time view of your spending. You can see where your money is going and make adjustments as needed. This feature is especially useful for identifying recurring expenses and subscriptions that you may have forgotten about.

Categorizing Transactions

Ensure that transactions are categorized correctly to get an accurate picture of your spending. Most apps allow you to review and adjust categories as needed. Regularly check your transaction history to verify that expenses are categorized correctly and make any necessary changes.

Proper categorization helps you understand your spending habits and identify areas where you can cut back. It also ensures that your budgets are accurate and that you are making informed financial decisions. Take the time to review your transactions and ensure that they are categorized correctly.

Monitoring Spending Patterns

Use the app's reporting features to monitor your spending patterns. Look for trends and identify areas where you can cut back or adjust your budget. Regularly reviewing your spending patterns helps you stay on track with your financial goals and make informed decisions.

Analyzing spending patterns can reveal insights into your financial habits. For example, you may find that you are spending more on dining out than you realized. Use this information to make adjustments and align your spending with your financial priorities.

CHAPTER 7: MASTERING BUDGETING

Setting Up Monthly Budgets

Create monthly budgets for different spending categories based on your financial goals and spending habits. Regularly review and adjust these budgets to stay on track. Setting up budgets helps you allocate resources efficiently and ensures that you are living within your means.

Budgeting involves setting limits for various categories, such as groceries, entertainment, and transportation. Use historical spending data to set realistic limits and adjust them as needed. The app will track your spending against these limits and provide feedback on your progress.

Adjusting Budgets Based on Goals

As your financial situation and goals change, adjust your budgets accordingly. This may involve increasing savings goals, reducing spending in certain areas, or reallocating funds. Regularly reviewing and adjusting your budgets ensures that they remain relevant and effective.

Financial goals can change over time, and your budgets should reflect these changes. For example, if you receive a raise, you may choose to allocate more money to savings or investments. Adjusting your budgets based on your goals helps you stay on track and achieve your financial objectives.

Using Alerts and Notifications

Set up alerts and notifications to help you stay on track with your budgets. Receive reminders for upcoming bills, alerts for overspending, and notifications for budget updates. Alerts and notifications provide timely feedback and help you stay on top of your finances.

Notifications can help you avoid overspending and ensure that you pay bills on time. Set up alerts for key events, such as when you are close to your budget limit or when a bill is due. This feature helps you stay proactive and avoid financial surprises.

CHAPTER 8: ADVANCED FEATURES AND CUSTOMIZATION

Goal Setting and Savings Plans

Use the app's goal-setting features to create savings plans for specific objectives, such as an emergency fund, vacation, or major purchase. Track your progress and stay motivated to achieve your goals. Setting clear financial goals provides direction and purpose for your financial activities.

Goals can be short-term or long-term, and your app can help you track progress towards these goals. For example, you may set a goal to save a certain amount each month for a vacation. The app will track your contributions and show you how close you are to reaching your goal.

Investment Tracking

Many financial apps offer investment tracking features, allowing you to monitor your portfolio's performance and make informed investment decisions. Track your investments alongside your expenses and budgets to get a comprehensive view of your financial health.

Investment tracking helps you stay informed about your portfolio and make strategic decisions. Monitor the performance of your investments and adjust your portfolio as needed. This feature provides valuable insights and helps you achieve your long-term financial goals.

Reporting and Analytics

Generate detailed reports and analyze your financial data to gain deeper insights into your spending and budgeting habits. Use these reports to make data-driven decisions and improve your financial management. Reports can highlight trends, identify areas for improvement, and provide a clear picture of your financial health.

Regularly review your financial reports to stay informed about your finances. Look for patterns and trends that can inform your financial decisions. Reporting and analytics provide a data-driven approach to financial management, helping you make informed choices and achieve your goals.

CHAPTER 9: MAINTAINING YOUR FINANCIAL HEALTH

Regular Reviews and Adjustments

Regularly review your financial data and make adjustments as needed. This helps ensure that you stay on track with your budgets and financial goals. Set aside time each month to review your finances and make any necessary changes.

Regular reviews help you stay proactive and address any issues before they become problems. Review your budgets, spending patterns, and financial goals to ensure that they are aligned with your overall financial plan. Make adjustments as needed to stay on track.

Managing Debt and Loans

Use your financial app to manage debt and loans. Track payments, monitor interest rates, and develop a plan to pay off debt efficiently. Managing debt is crucial for maintaining financial health and achieving long-term financial goals.

Develop a debt repayment plan that aligns with your financial goals. Use the app to track your progress and make adjustments as needed. Focus on paying off high-interest debt first and consider strategies such as debt consolidation to simplify your repayment process.

Planning for Major Expenses

Plan for major expenses by setting aside funds in advance. Use your app's budgeting and goal-setting features to allocate money for large purchases, such as a new car or home renovation. Planning ahead ensures that you are financially prepared for major expenses.

Major expenses can have a significant impact on your finances, so it's important to plan ahead. Set up a savings plan for large purchases and track your progress. Planning ahead helps you avoid financial stress and ensures that you have the resources you need.

CONCLUSION

Recap of Key Points

Expense tracking and budgeting apps offer powerful tools for managing your finances. By automating expense tracking, simplifying budgeting, and providing detailed financial insights, these apps can help you achieve better financial health and reach your financial goals.

Using a financial app provides a structured approach to managing your finances. Automated tracking, budgeting, and goal-setting features help you stay organized and make informed decisions. Regularly reviewing your finances and making adjustments ensures that you stay on track.

Encouragement to Utilize Financial Apps

Take the first step towards better financial management by choosing and implementing an expense tracking and budgeting app that fits your needs. Experience the benefits of automated tracking, improved budgeting, and enhanced financial awareness.

Financial apps provide valuable tools and insights to help you manage your finances effectively. By using these tools, you can achieve your financial goals and improve your overall financial health. Start using a financial app today and take control of your finances.

APPENDIX

Frequently Asked Questions

Glossary of Terms

www.ingramcontent.com/pod-product-compliance
Lightning Source LLC
Chambersburg PA
CBHW071222240526
45470CB00018B/2290